12 Steps To

Getting Admitted into Colleges & Universities in the United States

12 Steps To Getting Admitted into Colleges & Universities in the United States

Dr. Ohene Aku Kwapong

iUniverse, Inc.
New York Lincoln Shanghai

12 Steps To Getting Admitted into Colleges & Universities in the United States

All Rights Reserved © 2003 by Songhai Group

No part of this book may be reproduced or transmitted in any form or by any means, graphic, electronic, or mechanical, including photocopying, recording, taping, or by any information storage retrieval system, without the written permission of the publisher.

iUniverse, Inc.

For information address:
iUniverse, Inc.
2021 Pine Lake Road, Suite 100
Lincoln, NE 68512
www.iuniverse.com

First Edition

No part of this book may be reproduced in any form without a written permission from Songhai, except in the case of brief quotations embodied in articles and reviews.

ISBN: 0-595-29647-5

Printed in the United States of America

To my niece, Miriam, who gave me a reason to complete this book and offered herself as an example of the success that the book inspires in others.

CONTENTS

STEP 1 -	THE VISION AND THE PASSION	1
STEP 2 -	WHY APPLY TO SCHOOLS IN THE U.S.?	3
2.1	The College Experience: Taking control of your future	3
2.2	The pursuit of excellence	4
2.3	Better opportunities to accomplish goals	4
2.4	The Liberal Arts Experience	7
STEP 3 -	WHAT ARE THEY LOOKING FOR?	9
3.1	Areas To Differntiate Yourself	10
STEP 4 -	THE COLLEGE SEARCH: Identifying your schools	13
STEP 5 -	THE APPLICATION PROCESS	17
5.1	Drawing Up The Target List	17
5.2	Requesting Application Materials	19
5.3	Taking The Exams	20
5.4	Applying To Your Schools	23
STEP 6 -	EXCELLING AT THE SAT	27
6.2	Taking The SAT Again	30
STEP 7 -	SELLING YOURSELF TO THE DECISION-MAKERS	31
7.1	Recommendation Letters	31
STEP 8 -	COMPLETING YOUR APPLICATION PACKAGE	35
8.1	The Application Fee/Fee Waiver	35
8.2	The Main Application for Undergraduate Admission	36
8.3	Recommendations	37
8.4	Test Scores	38
8.5	Essays	39
8.6	Specific Requirements	40
8.7	Supplemental Materials	40
STEP 9 -	PAYING FOR YOUR FUTURE	41
9.1	Financing your University or College Education	41
9.2	Determining your financial need	41
9.3	What are the components of financial aid?	42
9.4	Sources of Financial Aid	43
STEP 10 -	BEFORE YOU APPLY: The financial paperwork	47
10.1	Filling Out The Forms	48
10.2	Financial Aid Resources	54
STEP 11 -	THE INTERVIEW AND THE FOLLOW-UP	57
11.1	The Interview	57
11.2	The Follow Up	59

STEP 12 - THE FINAL DECISION 63
    12.1   The Big Fat Envelope Or The Thin One 63
    12.2   The Award Letter 64
PUTTING IT ALL TOGETHER 67
APPENDIX - Worksheets 69
    Creating Target List 69
    Follow-up Sheet for Tracking Progress 70

- STEP 1 -
THE VISION AND THE PASSION

Get a vision for your life and what you want to accomplish

If you are reading this book, you have made a great decision. You desire to make the best of your college or university application process. You are probably excited, nervous and anxious, all at the same time, at the prospect of being a college student. Well, relax. Many students before you have survived this long, arduous process. With the right tools for a great application, you will find the best place to spend the next few years of your life.

This book is designed to make the whole application process a less intimidating one. As you read through each section, you will realize that the college application process is more than what meets the eye, but you will soon be on your way to a smooth application process, a journey that will be successful for you.

Every great journey begins with a vision. Without a clear vision for your life and goals to achieve that vision, you are bound to wander aimlessly from school to school, program to program, and you risk being disappointed on your day of graduation—when you should be happiest. Getting admitted to the school you choose begins with a vision that can be realized, a vision that puts you on that college or university campus of your choice.

My vision began with a picture of a cyclotron that I found in one of my middle school physics book. It was the small inscription—*Courtesy of MIT Nuclear Laboratory*—that gave birth to my vision of pursuing my first degree at MIT. It was that vision that led me into Professor Allotey's office at the University of Science and Technology, Ghana, West Africa, on one fateful afternoon in 1980 to ask him for a recommendation letter on my behalf to Princeton University, the Massachusetts Institute of Technology (MIT), and Dartmouth College. That same vision led me into the office of a Justice official, Appatu Plange, a former high court judge, to request my second recommendation letter. That vision was ultimately realized the day I joined the MIT Nuclear Engineering PhD program and took a stroll down Ames Street in Cambridge, MA, to see the cyclotron.

For my younger brother, who also completed his electrical engineering at MIT, the vision began with his passion for electronics and everything Sony. At a very early age he developed an interest in semiconductors and electrical systems. That interest led to a passion for the field that led to his applying for admission at MIT. His vision was realized the day he got a job at Sony-Asehi, managing a semiconductor production facility in the US.

For my niece, Miriam, her vision was rooted in her admiration for Madeline Albright and Hillary Clinton, and a desire to become like them. That vision was followed by a passion that led her to apply to Cornell University, Wellesley College (Hillary Clinton's alma mater), Swarthmore College, Barnard College and many others. She got admitted to every single school she applied to with fully funded scholarships. The reality of her vision began the day I gave her an autographed copy of Madeline Albright's memoir, *Madam Secretary*, addressed to her.

This book is about the critical steps that set her successfully on the path to achieving her vision. These same critical steps have provided the guidance for many others who have applied to US universities from either their home countries or other parts of the world and successfully gained admissions to US universities. While the 12 steps in this book are applicable for both domestic and foreign applicants, some of the information has been made specific to foreign applicants from places like Ghana for illustrative purposes.

Without a vision and the passion to see through the 12 steps, it is highly probable that you will not be successful in getting admitted to a college or a university in the US anytime soon. So, the first thing you need to do is to determine what your vision is or will be and get a sense of where that vision should begin.

TO-DO ITEMS:

Take about ½ a day, talk to your parents, guardian or someone you have enormous respect for, and answer the following 3 questions at the end of that day.

- Which of your interests and passions inspire you to be great?
- What is the one thing you believe you can do better than your classmates?
- Which individual, activity, idea, or image captures the essence of what you wish to become?

Discussing these questions with the people who know you well can help you craft a vision statement to help you tell your story as a prospective applicant.

- STEP 2 -
WHY APPLY TO SCHOOLS IN THE U.S.?

You need the best-fit academic experience to realize your vision

2.1 THE COLLEGE EXPERIENCE: TAKING CONTROL OF YOUR FUTURE

As you begin to reflect on your college plans, it is important to first think about what you want for your life. Where do you see, or where would you like to see yourself 5 years from today? While it may be difficult to have a definitive answer, you quickly begin to think about the things you enjoy doing and the interests you have. Your interests and passions will likely determine your career 5 years from today, and ultimately will determine where you spend the next four years of your life building that career.

Everyone student has a distinct path in life to follow; even though that path may look similar to what others have gone through. Some students arrive at college with a clear idea of what career they would like to pursue, while others arrive without a clue. Then there are the few who arrive with passions to pursue or a vision to discover new passions to pursue. It is this latter group that you should become a part of. The decision to go to college or university is more that just an endeavor to further your education; it is a first step towards developing your passion into a life-long endeavor that will define what you stand for. College is where you take control of your future to shape it the way you want and to take it where you want it to go. It is about making your vision become a reality.

Imagine this; before college you wanted to be a financial analyst. In your first year of college you took a lot of courses and decided you wanted to study marine biology. Along the way you became interested in social law, and at the end of your college career you decided to be a part-time social activist. Is this what college is all about? Yes and no. College is about several things: finding out more about yourself, developing your vision of your future, exploring new fields of knowledge, and discovering new paths in life that will lead to fulfilling passions on which careers are founded. It is the place where you will have the power to decide what your future should be.

On your day of graduation, you would have acquired skills and talents that are invaluable to the world beyond, gained a sense of what you can accomplish, and most of all, you would have taken control of *your* future and be in the most excellent position to make your vision a reality.

2.2 THE PURSUIT OF EXCELLENCE

If there is one word that captures the experience of attending a US college or university, it is *excellence.*

US colleges are unique in the sense that they provide both the competitive atmosphere and the challenging experiences that make it possible for you to develop a penchant for excellence. In such college environments, you will be challenged to make the best use of the resources available to you and be able to accomplish the goals you set for yourself. Without the environment to pursue excellence, your vision might as well be a half-baked dream that gets flushed down the drain. You have to make a decision to make the pursuit of excellence the hallmark of everything you do if your vision for your future is going to be realized.

2.3 BETTER OPPORTUNITIES TO ACCOMPLISH GOALS

College education in the US presents an opportunity that is unrivaled anywhere in today's world. Because of the large investments the US makes in education, there are many excellent colleges and universities that have trained many visionaries to become great leaders in either corporations or countries. There is no other individual society that can provide you with the uniqueness of opportunity that the US does.

So, as you begin to consider your vision and the goals you want to accomplish, recognize that the US has a unique advantage in the many opportunities available to help you pursue your vision. Just consider the following qualities that are unique to US colleges:

a) The Flexibility

Many colleges and universities in the US allow you the opportunity to distinguish yourself the way you want to, in any field of endeavor you choose. For instance, you can design your own course of study, take courses that tailor an academic program to your needs, and be able to engage in multi-disciplinary studies without restrictions often found in foreign universities. You can actively be involved in extracurricular activities, such as college sports, and still be good academically. You can start a literary publication, engage in athletic competitions, take part in radio production, or create a club of your own without anyone harassing you. The possibilities are endless.

b) Internships & Practice

You gain practical insight into subjects you take because most schools emphasize practicality and adopt a hands-on approach to learning. There are many research opportunities available, and independent learning is fostered. In addition, US colleges team up with companies to offer internship opportunities during the later years in college. These internships give you a chance to test out your career interests. For instance, I was able to test out career interests I had during several summers of internships at W.R. Grace & Co. in Boston, General Electric in New York, and Bethlehem Steel in Pennsylvania, before I finally decided that nonlinear systems and system dynamics were the areas in which I had the strongest interests.

With these internships, you are likely to develop relevant skills that you would otherwise not have had the opportunity to develop. If these skills are in an area about which you are passionate, that can give you an edge on the job market and set you on a path to starting your own business.

c) Access to the latest facilities

One great feature of schools in the US is the availability of modern facilities with the latest technologies. With these facilities you have continual access to information technology to build skills that will always keep you ahead of the rest of the world. You have access to networked classrooms and dorms. In addition to all these, most colleges have great library and athletic facilities. With colleges that are in close proximity to each other, you are able to cross-register for courses offered at other colleges and expand your course selection, as well as the resources available to you. While at MIT, I had the opportunity to take many of my courses at Harvard. The set of courses taken at Harvard set the stage for my later transition from an engineering career to a career in finance.

d) Global perspectives

Most US colleges also offer an approach to education with an international dimension, where global issues are part of the curriculum and broader perspectives are an essential part of your college experience. Study-abroad programs are very common and can provide an experience in education without borders. There is even a possibility that you might have access to internship and job opportunities abroad that might lead to careers in the international arena.

Chances are, you will be able to study in an environment that is more culturally diverse than you can find anywhere outside the US and be able to take advantage of developing a broader way of looking at issues that is bound to serve you well in a globalized world.

e) Relationships and a network for life

College may seem very far away from home and all the people you love. You may get a little homesick sometimes, but remember that college is place where you will develop long-lasting friendships with not only your college peers, but also with your professors and tutors.

There are orientation programs during your first few days at college to help you deal with issues on immigration, employment policies and regulations, and to help you adjust to campus life. For international students, there are various programs designed to help you adjust to living in the US. One particular program often offered to international students is the "Host Family Program." I was fortunate enough to have two host families during my years at MIT. One family—the O'Brien's—was more involved in Boston politics, while the other—the Whitman's—was more of a science family, with the father a weapons systems researcher at MIT's Draper laboratory. These two families later became invaluable and critical components of my college experience.

Most colleges also offer career counseling workshops designed to help you continuously evaluate your future plans and develop job search strategies as you approach graduation. You will have faculty mentors and advisors who will work closely with you within your field of study and help you navigate the complexities of campus life with confidence.

2.4 THE LIBERAL ARTS EXPERIENCE

What *is* the liberal arts experience? The concept of a liberal arts education is unique to US colleges and universities and revolves around an educational experience that is not limited to one traditional subject of study. The liberal arts experience gives you the opportunity to have a broad and balanced education, one often referred to as a "well-rounded" educational experience. If you desire a college education with a strong foundation, the liberal arts experience is worth your while. What you will discover is that the liberal arts experience gives you the foundational tools, as you seek out your future, to:

- Think critically about issues
- Develop an attitude that enables you to create and develop ideas.
- Develop critical writing and speaking skills
- Develop effective problem-solving skills
- Learn what it is you are passionate about and follow after it
- Explore an array of disciplines with a broad range of thinking
- Make connections between things that are seemingly unrelated
- Develop self-awareness and sensitivity to the needs of others in society
- Express yourself clearly and confidently
- Ask questions and seek answers
- Open yourself to new worlds of thought and imagination

To function effectively within the framework of today's increasingly complex global economy requires a broad understanding of many subject areas where seemingly unrelated things are interrelated. The liberal arts experience is essential to such a well-balanced education because it liberates the mind from a narrow focus.

The choice is yours. Do you want the liberal arts experience, and do you think it is worth your while? It is entirely up to you.

TO-DO ITEMS:

- Write down the one sentence that describes your vision
- Which of these are critical to making your vision a reality?
    1. A network of friends
    2. Excellence
    3. Control
    4. Liberal Arts Experience

- STEP 3 -
WHAT ARE THEY LOOKING FOR?

Determine what is needed for you to effectively get your vision across

Before you begin your college application process, ask yourself what it is that colleges, universities, and other institutions of learning seek. And keep in mind—*they want to know:*

- Can this student work effectively here?
- Does this applicant match our student profile and the programs we provide?
- Can this applicant actively and effectively contribute to our community, and in what ways?

A prerequisite to every institution of learning is a strong academic foundation and an adequate educational preparation. Your academic success in college will depend a lot on how well you fared in secondary or high school. Admission officers of the various colleges to which you are applying will spend quite some time reviewing and evaluating your school record. Their evaluation will be based on:

- your transcript
- your extracurricular commitments
- work experience
- volunteer work
- your essays
- community participation
- talent/ability
- character and personal qualities
- your vision and passion
- recommendations
- your standardized test scores (SAT I or ACT and SAT II)
- your course preparation
- an interview, if necessary

The admissions officers will want to know more about who you are. They would like to know about your views, values, aspirations, and experiences.

They would also like to know about your activities and interests, how you spend your time, and what is important to you. They will assess your strengths and abilities, as well as review what your teachers say about you in their recommendations. As they review your application, they will be searching for answers to these questions:

- What do you have to offer?
- Are you adequately prepared to contribute to and benefit from their community?
- Do your interests match their strengths?
- Do you have the vision and passion to make a difference?

In the end, they will compare you to several other students who are also applying for admissions. Your goal is to seek to differentiate yourself from the other applicants.

3.1　AREAS TO DIFFERNTIATE YOURSELF

3.1.1　*Academic Promise*

They look for academic achievement and outstanding scholarship. They look for accomplishment and the consistency with which you worked throughout secondary or high school. They will assess the strength of your curriculum and your academic standing, relative to your peers, or your rank in your class. They will search for answers to questions such as:

- Have you taken challenging courses, even at the cost of receiving a lower grade?
- Did you take advance placement, honors, or International Baccalaureate courses?
- Do you have a strong course selection, and what are the grades you have received?

3.1.2　*Resourcefulness*

Your academic record will be considered in light of the opportunities that were available to you in secondary or high school and the ways in which you made use of those opportunities.

Colleges want students who can best take advantage of the opportunities they offer, so make it clear that you realize these unique opportunities and show how best you will use them. Admissions officers will seek to find out whether you have taken the fullest advantage of what was available to you in your school or in your community.

3.1.3 Character Counts

You are who you are, and that is what makes you unique. Do not be hesitant to let your best qualities be expressed throughout the application process.

The admission officers search for qualities in applicants that will allow them to work well within their college communities. They seek out qualities such as confidence, curiosity, energy, seriousness, resilience, high motivation, and strong self-discipline. They look for all sorts of people: intelligent, outgoing, funny, and challenging. The best way for admission officers to find out about your strong personal qualities is through your extracurricular commitments, your essays, work experience, recommendations, and interviews. In your essays, do well to express and present your thoughts clearly and concisely, and do not be afraid to show some sense of humor. You will be surprised; people often enjoy a good sense of humor.

3.1.4 Community Involvement

Admission officers will consider your potential to contribute to their communities. They will look for leadership potential, as demonstrated through activities in your school or community. They will look for participation in school clubs and organizations, active participation in community service programs, and in volunteer work. Be as specific as possible when describing your involvements; they want to see exactly how you have challenged yourself beyond the classroom.

3.1.5 Talent/Ability

Do you write poetry or short stories? Do you write plays? Can you play an instrument? Are you an artist?

Your unique talent will distinguish you from other applicants and make it easier for admissions officers to take special note of you. This is your only chance to get the colleges to realize the great potential you offer.

In all these areas, you have an opportunity to differentiate yourself from the other applicants with whom you are competing. That should be easier to do in some aspects, since the areas in which you differentiate yourself revolve around your unique story and vision. To make these areas of differentiation credible and convincing to admission officers, you should provide some form of supplemental evidence to support these areas. Some of the supplemental documents that can be submitted along side your application can include certificates of achievements, awards, letters of recognition, and a portfolio of personal works.

TO-DO ITEMS:

Create a folder and put together a package with the following;
- All your secondary or high school transcripts
- All certificates of achievements
- Awards or letters of recognition
- Personal work: essays, artwork, etc.
- List out roles/responsibilities you had in clubs, organizations, or student government.

If there are areas of achievement or areas you believe will differentiate you but you do not have any supporting material, talk to someone who can attest to your abilities in those areas. Then ask them to write a letter of recognition on your behalf.

- STEP 4 -
THE COLLEGE SEARCH: Identifying your schools

Determine the academic environment that can bring the best out of you

Choosing where to actually spend the next few years of your life pursuing your college education is an arduous, long process, but it is the most critical step in your application process. The search for a school will not be overwhelming if you start with a clear vision and what you have to offer. In the end, you need to find a school where that vision will thrive—a school that buys into and shares your values, aspirations, goals and sense of purpose.

As you look at various colleges, make an effort to determine the things that are unique to that school, such as the culture and traditions. Those intangible qualities ought to be considered separately from the tangible things, such as college size, location, and costs. Here are some of the things worth considering in your search for a suitable college:

4.1.1   *Size*

Do you feel more comfortable in a small college, large university, or perhaps something in-between? Would you prefer a small undergraduate experience characterized by a small class size, a low student-to-faculty ratio, and greater personal attention and access to faculty? Or would you rather be part of a larger community with greater independence and cutting-edge research facilities typical of larger campuses?

4.1.2   *Type of School*

Do you want to attend a co-ed or single-sex institution? Do you prefer a college with which you can identify culturally, for instance a predominantly black college? Perhaps you would like to attend a college with a specific religious affiliation?

4.1.3   *Location*

Do you prefer a rural or an urban community? Does the surrounding community offer great opportunities? Do students get along with the neighboring communities? Do you want to be close to home, if you reside in the U.S.?

4.1.4 Curriculum

What is your intended major, and does the college have strengths in this area? What field(s) do you intend to pursue—something in Arts or Sciences, Engineering, Education, Law, Medicine, Business? Do you desire pure liberal arts, technical, or professional degree? Does the college offer the global perspectives your desire? Is there creative freedom? Can you design you own major and explore multiple fields of study?

4.1.5 Faculty

Do you want professors to play an active part in your life and help you make some important choices? Do you want to be taught by teachers who are well-published in their respectively fields, or ones with a generalized background? Do you want to learn from teachers who will inspire and challenge you? Do you want to have a personal, one-on-one relationship with your professors? Would you like to do collaborative research with your teachers? Are the professors mostly researchers, or just most part-time lecturers? Are classes mostly taught by professors or teaching assistants?

4.1.6 Student Body/Social Scene

Do students like having too much fun (party freaks), or are they intensely studious? Would you like to be part of a close-knit community where you can blend in and work to accomplish common goals and purposes? Would you like to belong to a community which places its emphasis on personal development? Is a diverse student body—where you cherish and value differences—of significance to you? Will the community be a place of intellectual stimulation for you? Do fraternities and sororities dominate the social scene? Educational institutions are often defined by their student body, so look into this thoroughly.

4.1.7 Extracurricular Life

What are some of your hobbies and interests *outside* the classroom? Are you a very athletic person? Consider the surrounding area. Are you a frequent beach-goer, or do you enjoy the great outdoors? What are some great spots for enjoyment and relaxation? Are you interested in community service or living a life devoted to social activism?

4.1.8 Resources

Does the college have the facilities you desire? Is there adequate access to these facilities? Is there a placed emphasis on interactive learning? Do you want to be able to conduct intensive research without much of a hassle?

4.1.9 Housing/Dining Services

What are the types of on-campus housing options? How many people live in one room? Will you commute (be a day student)? What are your dining options? How good is the food?

4.1.10 Job and Gradate Placement

What level of degree would you like to pursue? What percentages of students go off to graduate school? How extensive is the alumni network? Does the job-placement rate speak well of the school? Do you desire a professional or pre-professional type of preparation?

4.1.11 Admission Requirements/Procedures

Can you fulfill all of the school's admission requirements? Read about what aspects of your application are considered most important to the schools and about information concerning admission processes. For instance, do they give special consideration to minority students? Also, it's a good idea to keep in mind the level of selectivity, admission rates, percentage of international students accepted, and number of countries represented by the student body.

4.1.12 Financial Aid/Costs

Can you afford this particular institution? If cost is a major factor in your choice of schools, you will need to do some research on various costs and tuitions, as well as financial aid policies. Does the college offer financial aid to international students? What types of scholarships are available?

Gather up enough information about the various colleges you are interested in and narrow down your choices. It is generally a good idea to explore many sources of college information in order to make a well-informed choice.

There are a great number of resources available to help you with your college search, like various college publications; the *Princeton Review* is a great source of detailed college information. You can find out about numerous colleges and universities. Under each you will find information on the school's environment, various ratings, popular majors, financial aid information and much more.

You can find guidebooks of all sorts, as well as many electronic databases that will help you with your search. There are search databases that can actually conduct college searches for you. Take *Princeton Review's* www.review.com for instance, this electronic database allows you to build a personalized list of colleges just by indicating what exactly you are looking for in terms of location, preferred major, climate, etc. Chances are you will get a good list of colleges that match your personalized criteria.

You may also get advice from college counselors and advisors, as well as from family and friends. The United States Information Services Center is another invaluable source of information. There is so much information out there; you just have to know where to find it.

Remember; do not let others decide for you what you want. After all, you're the one going off to college, so take control of your college search. Of course it does not hurt to listen to the impressions of others. Just evaluate everything carefully.

TO-DO ITEMS:

- Determine the profile for the school characteristics you prefer. Assign a rating for the following characteristics: 1 for a must-have characteristic, 0 for a characteristic that is not important to you, and -1 for a characteristic you do not want.

SCHOOL CHARACTERISTICS	YOUR RATING
Size	
Type of school	
Location	
Curriculum	
Faculty	
Social Scene	
Extracurricular life	
Resources	
Admission Requirements	
Financial Aid / Costs	

- STEP 5 -
THE APPLICATION PROCESS

Select the schools with the qualities to make a difference in your life

5.1   DRAWING UP THE TARGET LIST

Now that you have considered your ideals and researched your college choices, it is time to narrow down those selections. Choose no more than eight (8) schools to research further—and apply to. It is a good idea to choose three selective schools that are likely to admit you, two that are very likely to admit you, and two to three schools that are sure to offer you admission (these are often referred to as "safety schools").

A good way to narrow the field for the schools that meet your criteria is to use the form provided below. This form helps you compare your rating of the schools on each of the qualities to the rating for your preference.

	Schools					My Preference
	Stanford	University of Wisconsin	Wellesly College	Columbia University	Dartmouth College	
Size	4	4	3	3	3	0
Type of School	3	2	3	3	3	0
Location	2	3	1	3	3	1
Curriculum	3	4	2	4	3	0
Faculty	3	4	2	4	2	0
Student Body, Social Scene	2	3	3	4	2	-1
Extracurricular Life	2	3	1	4	2	1
Resources	3	3	1	4	2	0
Admission Requirements	2	2	3	4	2	0
Financial Aid/Costs	1	3	3	4	3	1
Overall Score						

The next step is to duplicate the form above and generate a new number for each box by multiplying your preference rating by the corresponding school rating. The overall score for a particular school is the sum of all scores for the school.

	Schools				
	Stanford	University of Wisconsin	Wellesly College	Columbia University	Dartmouth College
Size	0	0	0	0	0
Type of School	0	0	0	0	0
Location	2	3	1	3	3
Curriculum	0	0	0	0	0
Faculty	0	0	0	0	0
Student Body, Social Scene	-2	-3	-3	-4	-2
Extracurricular Life	2	3	1	4	2
Resources	0	0	0	0	0
Admission Requirements	0	0	0	0	0
Financial Aid/Costs	1	3	3	4	3
Overall Score	3	6	2	7	6

My Preference
1 – Must Have
0 – Not Important
-1 – Do Not Want

School Rating
4 – Excellent
3 – Very good
2 – Good Enough
1 – Not Favorable

Results in each box to the left are generated by multiplying your preference rating by the corresponding school rating. Overall score is the sum of all scores.

The schools that end up with high overall scores are the schools you want to have at the top of your target list of colleges to which you want to apply.

5.1.1 Apply Now Or Wait?

Once you have drawn up the target list, it's time to manage your time wisely. How many months do you have till you write the SAT? How well do you think you will perform on the SAT? Will you write the SAT in time for score reports to reach your schools by their specified deadlines? At this point in time you should have an idea of what the SAT is all about. Also, you should have assessed how well you think you will do.

Would you like to wait till you write the SAT before you apply to the schools of your choice, or are you confident that you will meet the SAT ranges of your chosen schools? This is entirely up to you, but you must consider the time factor involved. If you can write the SAT before you apply and still meet application deadlines, fine, but if this is not possible, just apply. Besides, your SAT score is not the final determinant in your gaining admission. As said previously, evaluation is based on the totality of your application. If you fall short of the required SAT range, do not fret. There is a lot more flexibility to admission procedures than your may realize.

5.2 REQUESTING APPLICATION MATERIALS

Once you have decided which schools appeal most to you, request in writing via mail or e-mail that you would like these schools to send you their undergraduate admission and financial aid application materials. Where these materials are not available yet, ask them to place you on their mailing lists for these application materials. Some schools may ask that you request these materials online at their websites. Be sure to indicate whether you are applying as an international student or as a U.S. citizen; there are usually different applications for candidates in these two categories. If you want more specific information about what each school has to offer, request that you be sent their college brochures and any other information packages that you think will be of use to you. These will come in handy as you complete your applications for admission.

Most schools' application materials are downloadable, and there are many whose applications can be completed and submitted online. The online application is by far the fastest way to complete your applications. However, consider all the options available and do what works best for you.

5.2.1 *Reviewing Application Materials*

Once you have all of your application materials, read through them carefully. Read through the brochures and get to know your schools well. Visit college websites and find out more about student life, academic life, admissions procedures, etc. At this point you should know exactly what you want.

5.3 TAKING THE EXAMS

5.3.1 The SAT

The Scholastic Assessment Test (SAT) is one of the most widely-used US college or university entrance exam.

The SAT I: Reasoning test is a three-hour, multiple choice test that is used to assess your verbal and mathematical reasoning abilities.

The SAT II: Subject test is a one-hour test that focuses on your ability to apply knowledge acquired in a particular subject area you have studied over a period of time.

5.3.2 Registering For the SAT

Once you have figured out the various SAT requirements of all of your colleges, it is time to register. Online, fax, and telephone registrations are not allowed in places like Ghana, so it is best to register by mail. Registration forms are found within the SAT Registration Bulletin, which can be obtained at various educational agencies like W.A.E.C. (West Africa Examinations Council) or U.S.I.S (United States Information Services). Registration bulletins can also be requested from the College Board. Alternatively, you may write to the College Board to request a copy of the registration bulletin:

College Entrance Examination Board
P.O. Box 592
Princeton, NJ 08540
U.S.A.

College Board ATP
P.O. Box 6200
Princeton, NJ 08541
U.S.A.

Test registration arrangements should be made about six weeks prior to your selected testing date to avoid delays in the delivery of your admission ticket. You may take either the SAT I or up to three subjects under the SAT II on one given test date. Both tests cannot be taken on the same test date, and you must register for each test separately.

It is advisable to register early in order to get your first choice for a test center—the place where you will take the SAT exam.

5.3.3 Sending Scores

Remember that the basic registration fee covers the cost of sending only four score reports to the schools of your choice. Each additional score reporting code number you indicate on the registration form will be an additional $6.50.

Each time you register to take a test, you must be sure to indicate the schools to which you want your score report sent, using the school's 4-digit reporting code number, even if you did this on a previous test registration. You may also send your score reports using the following:

- The correction form on your admission ticket
- The additional report request form that was mailed with your admission ticket. The cost for each additional report is $6.50.
- By phone using a credit card.

Scores usually take from 3–6 weeks to be reported to the schools you designated to receive your score reports. Copies of score reports are not considered official, and your applications will not be considered complete until admission offices receive your *official* score reports directly from the College Board or the appropriate testing agency. However, if score reports do not get to the schools in time to meet application deadlines, send copies of the score report that you received in the mail. This should be done so the schools can begin to process your application. Make sure, however, that an official copy of your score report follows from the appropriate testing agency.

(2) The SDQ: Student Descriptive Questionnaire

When completing the SDQ, pay close attention to the questions that ask you to indicate the total number years of high school courses you have taken or plan to take, your grade-point average, and your class rank. Pay attention also to questions that concern what type of college you plan to attend (a 2-year or 4-year college, co-educational or single-sex college, private or public), size of college, college environment, housing options, your intended major, and—most importantly—your citizenship status and nationality. Some of these questions may ask that you indicate more than one option if you choose, as your preferences may change or you may just be undecided.

Note that the responses to the above SDQ questions will be shown on your score report, and this will allow you to see how each college's profile matches your own profile. It also gives each college the chance to know a little about you. If you happen to register for another test date, make sure to update all the SDQ responses that might have changed.

5.3.4 Other Tests

5.3.4.1 TOEFL

If English is not your first language or you have not been schooled in English you are required to take the **Test of English as a Foreign Language (TOEFL)**. Admission officers use this to evaluate your verbal ability at the level of most international students whose first language is not English. So it's fair and square! If you have a weak verbal score and your first language is not English, rest assured, the TOEFL will give you a boost. The "TOEFL Bulletin" which includes a registration form, should be available at educational agencies, such as **W.A.E.C** (West Africa Examination Council) or **U.S.I.S.** (United States Information Services). If you are unable to obtain this bulletin, you may request one by writing to:

TOEFL
P.O. Box 6152
Princeton, NJ 08541
U.S.A.

*Register at least six weeks before the test date.

5.3.4.2 ACT

The **ACT** (**American College Test**) is another test for admission purposes and can be taken in place of the SAT I and SAT II for most colleges. The ACT, much like the SAT I, is primarily a multiple choice test, but it has a wider content than the SAT I with English, Reading, Math and Science reasoning sections.

Here is some important contact information for the various testing agencies:

Educational Testing Service (ETS)
Rosedale Road
Princeton, NJ 08541
609-921-9000
www.ets.org

ETS (Educational Testing Service) administers the SAT I and SAT II.

American College Testing Program
P.O. Box 313
Iowa City, IA 52243
319-337-1270
www.act.org

5.4 APPLYING TO YOUR SCHOOLS

5.4.1 *When To Apply*

Most schools fall into two categories of admission types.

- Rolling admission—Here there is no firm application deadline and applicants are accepted or denied until freshmen classes are filled.
- Selective admission—In this case, schools have postmark or priority-filing deadlines, which usually fall within the months of January and February.

Most people start applying to the schools of their choice within the first half of their senior year or after completing secondary school. Do what works best for you. However, it is best to begin preparing your applications by November and December and to complete them within these months.

5.4.2 *Decision Options*

There are various plans that colleges use in evaluating application materials. Here are the three basic plans that you should take note of:

- **Early Decision Plan**

The Early Decision Plan is designed for applicants who have thoughtfully and thoroughly investigated a favored college relative to their other college choices and have found it to be an indisputable first-choice. The Early Decision (ED) Plan is a binding agreement and commitment to a college that you would like to take first priority over your other college choices.

For the most part, under Early Decision Plans you may have no more than one Early Decision application underway at a time, and you may apply to other colleges only under their Regular Decision Plans. Check out all of your schools on their policies regarding the Early Decision option if you intend to apply under this plan. Under most Early Decision Plans you are required to accept if admitted (especially if you get a good financial aid offer), and withdraw all other applications. If you want to negotiate a very adequate financial aid bargain, it is wise not to apply under this plan, since other schools may offer you better bargains.

If you are not admitted under the Early Decision Plan, you may be deferred to the Regular Decision applicant pool or denied admission altogether (this withdraws your application from further consideration).

Also, keep in mind that for you to apply under the ED plan means that you must file your applications as early as October or November. Candidates under this plan are most likely to receive notification of admission decisions as early as December, so in order to meet early application deadlines you must take the required standardized tests early and be sure to have your scores reported directly to your college(s) by the appropriate testing agency in time to meet their application deadlines. You must also remember to file your financial aid applications earlier on to promptly meet financial aid deadlines.

- **Early Action Plan**

This plan is designed for applicants who do not want to commit to any particular college as their first-choice, but who would like to learn of their admission status early. Under this plan, most schools require that candidates apply as early as November, after which they will receive notification of admission decisions as early as January or February.

- Regular Decision Plan

This plan is designed for applicants who want to keep themselves open to several options throughout the application process. Under this plan, applications are usually filed in January or February and applicants usually receive notification of admission decisions early on in April.

5.4.3 How To Apply

What does the application process involve? Every school has its set of specific guidelines for application procedures, but they all generally follow the same pattern. Many colleges are now using what is called the **COMMON APPLICATION**, an eight-page undergraduate admission application form. There are about 200 colleges that endorse the use of the Common Application. If the schools you are applying to do not endorse the use of the Common Application, you will have to use their institutional-specific application forms.

You are welcome to use the paper version of the applications if you prefer. However, if you do have access to the Internet, and especially if mailing will pose a problem for you, as with our slow international mailing system, many schools now accept applications via online forms. At these online application sites you can visit numerous times to revise your application materials before submitting them. You may also have the option of applying online, printing out the application that you filled out online, and mailing it. Otherwise, you can submit the online application electronically.

Here are some application-related websites that you might like to visit:

- Apply! (http://www.weapply.com)
- College NET Apply Web (http://www.applyweb.com/aw/)
- College View AppZap (http://www.collegeview.com/appzap/)
- XAP College Admissions Applications Online (http://www.xap.com/xapwww/eduX.html)

5.4.4 The Common Application

As said previously, the Common Application is an eight-page undergraduate admission application form that you may use in place of institutional-specific applications. However, there are only about 200 schools that endorse its use, so check whether the schools you are applying to accept this form of application in place of their own institutional application before using it.

One advantage of the Common Application is that it only needs to be filled in once. Once it has been filled in, you may make copies of it and send them to the various schools to which you are applying. If you are applying to a college using the Common Application, you are also required to complete the college's application supplement, which is included in most college application booklets or sent directly to you upon receipt of your completed Common Application.

The Common Application may be downloaded, along with its corresponding college application supplement from the Common Application Organization website at http://www.app.commonapp.org/action/apply.nsf/. It can also be completed online at the following websites:

- http://www.apply.embark.com
- http://www.nextstopcollege@collegeboard.org/
- http://www.collegelink.com

*Make sure to check whether the colleges to which you are applying use the Common Application. Colleges that endorse its use are printed on the top of the first page of every Common Application form.

TO-DO ITEMS:

- Draw up your target list: the schools that meet the criteria for the environment you want.
- Choose a date to take the SAT or other required tests. Register for these tests at least 6 weeks in advance.
- Write to the schools to request application for admission forms and a school catalogue.
- For each of the schools, put together a folder. This is where you will keep copies of all correspondence and documents sent as part of your application.

- STEP 6 -
EXCELLING AT THE SAT

This is the one test you can excel at if you get passionate about it

The SAT is very important, and is unlike any other test you have taken in secondary or high school. Many students are intimidated by the sheer thought of taking the SAT. It is just a test, and fortunately, it is not a test of everything you have learned from primary school till now. It is simply a skill's assessment test that examines your knowledge of basic math and verbal concepts. For the SAT, there are no past questions that repeat themselves in every test. Sure, most of the question types follow the same pattern and test the same basic skills and concepts, but here you must learn to apply the knowledge you have acquired and use strategy in solving problems and answering questions.

Colleges use the SAT as a standard measuring stick to compare students from different educational systems around the world. It is intended to measure the aptitude of each individual.

Every college has its own way of evaluating an applicant. Some may be of the opinion that SAT scores are vital in making an admission decision, and some may not even require the SAT to make a decision. The SAT is just one piece of the puzzle in admission requirements, so do not think it is the final determinant.

6.1.1 *Tips for SAT preparation*

It is a good idea to study at least 2 months before the exam so you are well acquainted with the structure of the SAT and all the strategies employed in conquering the test.

There are many SAT studying materials and books available to help prep you on specific question types and strategies applied throughout the SAT. A lot of these study materials also have SAT practice exams you can try your hands on.

Practice sample SAT tests under timed conditions. This will give you a sense of the 3-hour testing experience and help you estimate how you will fare on the real exam. Don't get discouraged if you take a practice test and get a low score; monitoring your progress and improving upon your strengths and weaknesses should be your main focus.

Make sure that as you try out the practice tests you watch carefully where you shade. Be certain that the number you are answering on the question sheet is the same as the number that appears on the answer sheet. Come test day, if you are shading the right answers to the wrong questions, chances are you will end up with a very low score. Also, be careful when you skip questions. If you skip a question, mark that question number on both your question paper and answer sheet. This makes it a lot easier to revisit unanswered questions. Try not to skip around too frequently within each section; in the real test, once you complete a section within a certain time limit you won't be allowed to return to it.

Familiarize yourself with all the question types and read the directions (which remain the same for every test) for each set of questions repeatedly so you remember them very well. Bear in mind that there is a time constraint in taking the SAT; so come test day; you will not want to waste time reading instructions with which you are already familiar.

All questions on the SAT are worth the same number of points. Nevertheless, with each set of question types (except critical reading questions), the level of difficulty gradually increases. Consequently, it is best to tackle the first set of questions (the area of least resistance, where it will pay off to spend your time) before moving on to the harder questions, which will inevitably take up more of your time. On the other hand, don't answer the easy questions so fast that you make careless mistakes and lose points that otherwise would have easily been gained. Also, try not to answer the simpler questions so slowly that less time is available to answer the harder questions that take up more of your time.

The SAT is scored over a total scale of 1600:800 for MATH and 800 for VERBAL. You gain one point for every question you answer correctly and lose a fraction of a point for every question answered incorrectly. Points are neither gained nor lost for omitted or unanswered questions.

As you answer the "all too familiar" multiple choice questions, keep in mind that guessing doesn't really hurt, but what is important is that you make an *educated* guess. This way you increase your odds of guessing correctly. Try making use of the "process of elimination" strategy. It always works.

You have tried your hands on some practice tests, to no avail. You have done question after question, and it seems like there's no end in sight. You feel like studying is a hassle. Aim at a good study plan. Find a quiet place where you can concentrate and where there are no distractions or disturbances. Have a timer, a clock, or a watch nearby so you can time yourself as you take the practice exams. (It is important to work under the time-simulated conditions.)

Develop a study plan that works for you. It is best to take a diagnostic test (a practice test taken without studying) before you start taking the real practice tests so you can examine yourself and know where your areas of strength and weakness lie. Learn as many test-taking strategies as you can, and practice, practice, practice! Try your hands on a lot of practice tests and continue to assess your strengths and weaknesses, especially problematic areas where you need to channel most of your energy. Remember to score yourself after each test in order to keep track of your progress. Lastly, set goals for yourself and achieve them!

As test day nears, you should try a lot of practice tests. Do less learning and more practicing. During the last phase of preparation, you should be familiarized with test-taking strategies, instructions, and the SAT as a whole; you should know exactly what to expect on test day. After all, the key to full-confidence on test day is, of course, being well-prepared. Invest a lot of time and effort into your SAT preparation and you won't be disappointed.

6.1.2 *The day before the test*

You open a book and you realize, "Wow! I haven't worked out this problem yet" and "Oh, I really need to get more vocabulary into my head" or "I still don't get this problem!" Relax. Chances are you're blowing things out of proportion. Rest your mind, go over a few more practice tests, and end it there. You might be tempted to do some cramming till the next morning.

This is not advisable. Last-minute cramming isn't going to do you much good. The SAT is more a test of how you think and strategize than what you know. Last-minute studying just might confuse or intimidate you even further. Find a diversion, like watching one of your favorite movies or playing a good game of basketball—anything to get your mind off the SAT.

Make sure you have everything you need for the test the night before:

1) A watch
2) A calculator (with fresh batteries)
3) 3 No. 2 pencils with erasers

4) Your admission ticket (sent to you in the mail).
5) Valid identification (valid passport, school I.D.)

Last but not least, get a good night's rest. This is the best solution for a well-prepared mind on test day.

6.1.3 Test day

Eat a good breakfast in the morning so your mind will be fully alert as you take the SAT. Also, make sure you have everything you need to take the test before you leave the house. Leave early for your test center so you don't arrive there late.

6.2 TAKING THE SAT AGAIN

Every school has its way of evaluating your performance on the SAT. Some may take your highest verbal and math scores if you have tested more than once. Some also may take your highest combined score from a particular test date. Other schools may very well average all of your combined scores.

Someone who takes the SAT for the first time and receives a score of 1260 is better off than another person who gets the same score after taking the SAT three times. Don't worry if the scores that you receive are not within the score ranges specified by the colleges that you intend to apply to. Most schools will not hold 20 points against you; if the minimum score requirement for one of your schools is say 1200 and you get a score of 1180, chances are they will not hold it against you. No one will deny you admission because you got about 2 more questions wrong on the SAT. Also, be rest assured that the SAT I, for example, has become much easier in recent years (see Table above).

Trends in Statistics on Admitted Students			
	1993	1998*	2003
SAT I			
One 800 score	14%	33%	36%
Two 800s	<1%	7%	8%
*SAT scores were re-centered in 1995, making it easier to attain an 800. Source: Technology Review			

If you really think that you didn't do too well and you would like to take the SAT again, or you just want to improve upon your score, that's fine. However, do not take the SAT a second time if you do not expect to score significantly higher the second time around.

- STEP 7 -
SELLING YOURSELF TO THE DECISION-MAKERS

The best advocates are willing to endorse your vision and aspirations

7.1   RECOMMENDATION LETTERS

A recommendation letter is a third-party testament or endorsement of your strengths and unique attributes, and therefore represents an independent opinion that could sway admission officers towards extending an offer to you. As a third-party testimonial, any effective recommendation letter has to have three basic elements:

- Credibility and Position of the recommender
- Independence of thought expressed by the recommender
- Clarity and Focus in scope in recommendation

Choose carefully the person you ask to write your recommendation letters for you. There are 3 areas to focus on when considering who to ask to write recommendations for you.

1. Academic Performance—The first recommendation should come from someone who is very familiar with your academic performance. We will suggest the following:

    a.   Headmaster, Headmistress or Principal
    b.   A teacher in your most excellent subject
    c.   A personal tutor who is very familiar with your academic strengths

The advice here is to go with a teacher or a personal tutor, since most Headmasters, Headmistress or Principals usually do not know you well enough to offer something compelling. In the absence of any of the above, you may consider having a separate individual—someone with a distinguished academic standing—outside of your school, or someone who can review your academic record and offer a compelling testament on your behalf. This is the most critical recommendation, so do not waste it on a recommender whom you doubt will offer a luck-luster testimony. Do whatever it takes to get the strongest academic recommendation possible, even if you have to provide the recommender with an outline of the strongest areas of your academic record to emphasize. I chose to ask Professor Allotey of the University of Science and Technology in Ghana to write my first recommendation. Why? Because he was then a visiting professor at Princeton University, had the credibility factor, and was willing to discuss with me my strongest academic areas of performance in order to offer an effective testimony.

2. Familiarity with your vision—The second recommendation is really a testimony from someone who is more of a mentor and knows about your passions, interests, and goals in life. The purpose of this recommendation is basically to let the admissions officers hear your story and vision from a third person. This recommendation has to look to the future and emphasize the things that make you unique, what you have to offer, and why the college could use someone like you.

3. Character Testament—The final recommendation usually comes from a guidance counselor, your favorite teacher, or someone who can tell the college about your character and the traits that have served you well. This is supposed to make you come across as personable, hardworking, and able to handle the challenges of human relationships. This one might well be written by your pastor or spiritual counselor.

Whoever you ask to write a recommendation for you, do not hesitate to ask them for a copy to review before it gets sent. If what they write is not very positive and does not meet the criteria above, do not submit it with your application.

7.1.1 Sample Recommendation Letter

February 5, 2003

RECOMMENDATION FOR MIRIAM T. OKINE

Dear Sir/Madam,

It is with much pleasure that I write on behalf of Miss Miriam T. Okine. I have known her for over 10 years and I continue to be amazed by her enthusiasm and ambition in seeking admission into your university.

Apparently, because of time constraints, it was impossible for her to complete the SATII and has submitted her national exam results in

STEP 7 - SELLING YOURSELF TO THE DECISION-MAKERS

lieu of that. I sincerely hope that will not be an insurmountable hurdle to her pursuit of excellence and aspirations.

Miriam has an incredible goal of becoming an economist and has often cited Madeline Albright as one her role models and end goal. It amazes me because, unlike most of the students educated in Africa, she has such clarity and focus with regard to what she wants to pursue. Her numerous writings, poems, and other essays (which often are done as a hobby) show a level of maturity that demonstrates an incredible level of comfort with the difficult issues of today.

I have personally made a promise to get her published when she completes a first set of poems that she wrote when she was just about 8 years old. I am happy to know that she has kept the same level of ambition and dedication in pursuing her academic studies.

Miriam will be a unique addition to your school, because as an individual contributor she is bound to make a major contribution and bring a perspective that I believe will emphasize excellence and scholarship in the pursuit of one's goal.

It is with sincere pleasure that I do recommend her for admission into your entering class.

Sincerely,
Dr. Ohene Kwapong,
Microsoft Corporation, 26/3375

TO-DO ITEMS:

Write down the names of the three individuals you believe can give you very good recommendation letters.

	Name	**Recommendation Focus**	**Position**	**Relationship**
Example	John D. Whitfield	Personal / Character	Professor	Alumni / Mentor
1)				
2)				
3)				

Be sure to ask these individuals, at least 6 weeks before application deadlines, to write recommendation letters on your behalf.

- STEP 8 -
COMPLETING YOUR APPLICATION PACKAGE

This package is the one story you get to live if it captures your vision

Here are the things you need to complete your application:

8.1   THE APPLICATION FEE/FEE WAIVER

The application fee is the fee that you pay along with your application for admission in order to cover the costs of processing your application. If the payment of the application fee would pose a financial burden for you or your family, you may request that the fee be waived by the college to which you are applying. In order to do this, enclose with your application a fee waiver: a letter explaining the circumstances surrounding your inability to pay the application fee. This fee waiver must be signed by your school counselor or an appropriate authority who is aware of your financial hardship.

Most schools will willingly accept the fee waiver, but some may not allow this. In that case, you must submit the required application fee. If it is difficult to submit the fee because of currency restrictions, it might be more convenient to request that a friend or relation in the U.S. submit the fee on your behalf.

8.1.1.1   Sample "Request for Fee Waiver" Letter

P.O. Box 2345
Accra, Ghana

December 12, 2002

Dear Sir/Madam,

REQUEST FOR APPLICATION FEE WAIVER

I would like to take this opportunity to request that the application fee be waived, if possible.

I realize there are several applicants probably requesting fee-waivers. Quite frankly, I do not think I am more deserving of a waiver than they are. However, I am currently financially burdened with two academic projects of personal interest. To enclose a check for the fee will be very difficult for me at this time. I seriously want my application for admission to be processed, so please do consider at least postponing the payment of the fee.

I hope you share my view that this should not prevent me from pursuing the opportunity of being a part of and contributing to the academic endeavors in your school.

Sincerely yours,

Miriam T. Okine
(Prospective Applicant)

8.2 THE MAIN APPLICATION FOR UNDERGRADUATE ADMISSION

When filling out your applications, make sure you fill in accurate information concerning your education, extra curricular and volunteer activities, work experience, family, and about yourself personally. These are very important.

Some colleges accept the Common Application in lieu of their own application and give equal consideration to either of them. These applications are available in paper or electronic form. Remember to attach your fee or fee waiver request to the main application so the admission officers can begin to process your application in time.

8.2.1 School Counselor's Report

This is the form that should be given to your secondary school or guidance counselor to be filled in and sent directly to the colleges to which you are applying. Attached to the school counselor's report should be your transcript and your final examination results (certified copies of these), as well as your mid-year report (if you are still in secondary school).

8.2.2 Transcript

The transcript is a written record of your academic performance in secondary school. It should indicate your cumulative grade-point average, rank in class (if available), and a grading scale. Certified or official copies of your transcript should be signed by an appropriate school official, then attached to the school counselor's report and submitted along with it.

8.2.3 S.S.C.E. Results/Final Examination Results

If you have completed secondary school, you must submit certified copies of your final examination results along with the school counselor's report, or ask the Examinations Council to mail confidential results to the colleges to which you are applying. Your final examination results will help admission officers evaluate how well you fared upon your completion of secondary school.

8.2.4 Mid-Year Report

The mid-year report form should be completed by your school counselor if you are still in secondary school. The mid-year report informs admission officers of your academic progress in the first half of your senior year in secondary school, so keep in mind that your senior year grades still count towards the completion of your application for admission. If, however, you are applying to college, having already graduated from secondary school, then you may disregard the mid-year report entirely.

After submitting your completed application, some schools may still write to you regarding a missing mid-year report. Contact these schools through electronic mail and explain to them that the mid-year report is not applicable to you since you have completed and are out of secondary school, and also that all the grades you obtained in secondary school are included in your school transcript. It is a good idea to write a formal explanation and mail this to the school also, just in case they do not receive the e-mail message on time.

8.3 RECOMMENDATIONS

Most colleges require that you submit two teacher recommendations or evaluations. Ask a teacher who has taught you in an academic subject—within the last two years of your secondary education—to complete a recommendation for you. In these recommendations, your teachers will give their appraisals of your contribution(s) to their classrooms and to the school community, as well as make mention of some of your noteworthy achievements.

Recommendations are very helpful to admission officers as they read about what various individuals have to say concerning you. In other words, your achievements, accomplishments, skills, talents, and strong characteristics are brought to light. In fact, it is a great idea to get additional letters of recommendation from teachers and professors who know you, as well as from employers and coaches (especially when you want colleges to know about your athletic capabilities). These may very well be of great advantage to your application.

8.3.1 Peer Evaluations

Some colleges may ask you to submit peer evaluations. In this case, ask a good friend of yours who has known you for quite a while to complete the required peer evaluation form and submit it to the colleges that require it.

8.4 TEST SCORES

Most schools will ask that you submit the results of the various tests that they require. For a number of schools, also, submitting test scores is completely optional.

Generally, all applicants are required to submit the results of the College Board's Scholastic Assessment Test—**SAT I: Reasoning Test** and **SAT II: Subject Test** (if required) or the American College Test (**ACT**). Applicants who are non-native speakers of English are advised to take the Test of English as a Foreign Language (**TOEFL**). Some schools may waive the TOEFL if you obtain a relatively high verbal score on the SAT. Check on admission policies concerning this.

Your test scores need to be on file for admission officers to fully process your application. Be sure to have your score reports sent directly from the appropriate testing agencies to the schools to which you are applying.

8.5   ESSAYS

Schools you apply to will require you to either write a number of essays or a personal statement. For those that require an essay, you will most likely be asked to evaluate a specific issue of importance to you, write about a specific experience that you have had, or describe how someone has influenced your life. Schools that use the Common Application and require an application supplement may ask that you also submit a supplemental essay in addition to a personal statement.

Use these essays to convey to the school *what really differentiates you from all the other students who are also applying* to the same school. What you ultimately put down on paper will reveal your passions and can help the decision-makers capture the vision you bring. When I completed my MIT application, I was asked to write a short essay (75-100) words on *Why do you want to study at MIT?* Quite frankly, I misunderstood the instructions to mean I could submit a portfolio of work, as an artist might submit for an art essay. As a result of my misunderstanding, I produced one of the most elaborate cartoon pieces I had ever done in my life. A 17x14" illustration that depicted an old man at the end of his life's journey with a selected list of engineering puzzles, arriving at the steps leading up to MIT's main rotunda, was my response to that simple question, *Why do you want to study at MIT?* I later found out what could have been a disqualifier for my essay submission turned out to be the one thing that distinguished me from many applicants.

Be creative with your essays, but only to the extent that brings out the vision to which you aspire. Write your essays with meaning and clarity, because admission officers are also looking out for applicants who express themselves well and have a command of the English language. Be specific when describing your personal experiences and do not write to your schools about facts they already know—like how great you think the student-faculty ratio is and the number of students that enroll there. They want to know about you. Essays give you the opportunity to present yourself in ways that your grades and standardized test scores alone cannot, ways that give them a sense of your vision and the passions that drive you. So, be you.

Be sure to write your name and date of birth on the pages of your essay for to make it easy for admission officers to keep track of your application.

8.6 SPECIFIC REQUIREMENTS

Various schools and majors may have their own requirements. For instance, most schools require potential music majors to submit audition tapes and prospective art majors to submit examples of their art work. Others may require special interviews. Just make sure you fulfill all the needed requirements for each of the schools to which you apply.

8.7 SUPPLEMENTAL MATERIALS

A lot of schools will take the time to review supplemental materials, like examples of personal expression, creative writing, and artwork that greatly enhance your application. Actually, most schools encourage the submission of supplemental materials, as these often give them the opportunity to appreciate, as well as assess, some of your strengths and talents.

Once again, do not forget to label these materials with your full name and social security number (if you have one) in order for admission officers to keep track of all of your application materials.

TO-DO ITEMS:

Below is a check-list of the items that need to be in the package to be submitted to the schools you are applying to.

- A cover letter
- Application fee or waiver request
- Completed application form
- Certified copies of transcripts
- Three recommendation letters
- Completed essays
- Photocopies of SAT/TOEFL/ACT results if available
- Certificates of achievements, letters of recognition or awards
- Portfolio of personal work
- OPTIONAL : Counselor's report
- OPTIONAL: SSCE, O'Level, A'Level or other national examination results

You should also request official copies of your test scores to be sent directly to the schools. Finally, the completed package should be mailed to the school at least 2 weeks before the application deadline.

- STEP 9 -
PAYING FOR YOUR FUTURE

Your future will be paid for if you have the passion and your vision is compelling

9.1 FINANCING YOUR UNIVERSITY OR COLLEGE EDUCATION

You are probably worried that the quality of education you need to realize your vision is beyond your reach financially. The rising cost of a college education might deter you from pursuing your college career. You ask yourself, *Can I afford this?* Well, rest assured. College is much more affordable than you might think. Of course the costs involved in going to college might seem overwhelming, but as costs have increased, so also have the range of financial aid resources available to help with the costs of college and make them more manageable.

View a college education as a long-term investment—one that appreciates in value as the years go by and creates a lifetime of great opportunity. It will probably be the biggest and most significant investment you will ever make in your future.

Many institutions have a "need-blind" policy concerning financial aid. This simply means that admission decisions are made regardless of your ability to pay for college. Don't think that by asking for financial assistance you are decreasing your chances of gaining admission to the colleges of your choice or that you are selling yourself short.

9.2 DETERMINING YOUR FINANCIAL NEED

Many tertiary institutions realize that families look beyond their own resources in catering for the cost of a college education, and they are willing to help out. In determining your financial need, most institutions use an eligibility formula for federal aid (Federal Methodology) and/or their own institutional methodology.

Financial need is basically determined by the cost of attending college minus your family's expected contribution: Expected Family Contribution or EFC. The EFC is the total amount that you and your family are expected to contribute towards covering the cost of your college education. The financial aid staff will take the time to review your overall financial circumstances and compare it to that of other families.

Your EFC is determined based on the information you and your family provide in your financial aid applications. Here are the factors that might be involved in determining your EFC:

- family income
- your income
- family assets
- your assets
- taxes paid for the year
- untaxed income
- money held in checking and savings accounts
- ownership or investments in a business or corporation
- basic expenditure and unusual expenses(medical or otherwise)
- size of family
- number of family members attending college
- elementary and secondary school tuition paid
- special circumstances

9.3 WHAT ARE THE COMPONENTS OF FINANCIAL AID?

Financial aid, which is the difference between your EFC and the cost of attending the school of your choice, is made up of the following components:

9.3.1 *Grants and scholarships*

These are gift aids which do not have to be repaid or maintained by work. Grants are usually awarded based on need, while scholarships are awarded to students who have met some institutional criteria; for instance, athletic scholarships awarded to students with exceptional athletic capabilities or merit-based scholarships awarded to students based on overall academic records and/or SAT and ACT scores or simply based on great community involvement. Grants and scholarships are available from a variety of sources like college gift and endowed funds, federal and state governments and outside agencies and organizations.

9.3.2 Loans

These are widely available from a variety of sources and must be repaid at required interest rates. For most loans, payment can be deferred until you complete college. Borrowing is a good idea, especially where you fall short of scholarship and grant aid.

9.3.3 Work study

This gives you the opportunity to earn college funds by working on and/or off campus during the academic year.

The financial aid staff at the colleges of your choice will work together with you to negotiate a financial aid package that may contain any combination of the above-mentioned components.

9.4 SOURCES OF FINANCIAL AID

Applying for financial aid is much like applying for admission into a college; it requires you to be meticulous. You must have an understanding of all the resources and options that are available to you.

9.4.1 Federal Aid

This is by far the largest source of financial aid available to U.S. citizens or permanent residents of the U.S. Through the department of Education (www.ed.gov) the government makes funds available to many students every year to help them bear the financial burden of paying for college. Here are some federal aid programs you should know about:

9.4.1.1 Federal Pell Grant

This is available to all eligible undergraduate students. Eligibility for this grant is determined by the standard Federal Methodology formula used to calculate your EFC (Expected Family Contribution). If your EFC falls below a certain threshold, you will be eligible for the Pell Grant. If you've applied for federal aid (by submitting the FAFSA), you'll receive a Student Aid Report (**SAR**) that will give you your EFC figure and tell you whether you have qualified for the Pell Grant or not. The amount of the grant that you may receive varies from school to school, but basically ranges from $400.00-$4,000.00 annually. Bear in mind that the application for the Pell Grant is the **Free Application for Federal Student Aid (FAFSA)**. No payment of the grant is possible until the results of your FAFSA application have been received by the federal processing agency.

9.4.1.2 Federal Stafford Loan

This is a long-term, low-interest educational loan available through banks or the federal government. Eligibility for a Stafford Loan is determined by the college to which you are applying, using certain federal guidelines. Family income and assets, family size, and number of children in college are all factors that determine your Stafford Loan eligibility if you intend to apply for financial aid.

If by federal regulation you are eligible for an interest subsidy, your Stafford Loan will be interest-free during your full-time enrollment in college, and the interest will be paid by the federal government. However, if you are not eligible for the interest subsidy, interest will accrue on your Unsubsidized Stafford Loan. Repayment of the Stafford loan can be deferred until you graduate from college. Interest rates are variable, but can not exceed 8.25%. The average loan amount given to freshmen is $2,625.00 annually.

9.4.1.3 Campus-based Financial Aid Programs

Some colleges administer the following financial aid programs:

a) <u>Federal Supplemental Educational Opportunity Grants (FSEOG)</u>
These grants are provided by the federal government to students who demonstrate exceptional financial need (with the lowest EFCs). Funds range from $100.00-4,000.00 annually.

b) <u>Federal Work-Study (FWS)</u>
This program allows students with financial need to earn money from a part-time job—provided by their college—towards educational costs. This is also a great opportunity to gain work experience, maybe even within a chosen field.

c) <u>Federal Perkins Loan</u>
This is a low-interest loan for students with exceptional financial need. Interest rates are fixed at 5% and repayment begins 9 months after graduation and continues for up to 10 years.

These programs have limited funds available, so make sure you apply for financial aid as early as possible.

9.4.2 State Aid

There are many state-sponsored grants and scholarships for which residents of certain states may be eligible. It is best to contact your state's scholarship or educational agency for more information concerning this.

9.4.3 Private scholarships and grants

Taking advantage of these funds is a good way to supplement inadequate financial aid resources and reduce debt caused by loan components. Here are some websites that offer free scholarship searches:

- CASHE—http://scholarships.salliemae.com/
- College Board—http://www.collegeboard.org/fundfinder/html/ssrchtop.html
- CollegeNET—http://www.collegenet.com/mach25/
- FastWEB—http://www.fastweb.com/
- FinAid Database—http://www.finaid.org/
- Scholarship Resource Network—http://www.srnexpress.com/execsrch.html

9.4.4 College funds

These funds usually consist of merit-based aid and do not need to be taken into account. With college funds, a lot of the financial aid that students receive is taken from college endowment funds.

TO-DO ITEMS:

- Determine a range for how much a full year will cost if you are admitted to the schools you selected.
- For each of your schools, find out the forms of financial aid that are available and which ones you can apply for.
- Request for Application for Financial Aid forms, if not included in the Application for Admission forms sent to you.

- STEP 10 -
BEFORE YOU APPLY: The financial paperwork

Focus on getting admitted and someone will pay for you to realize your vision

When I first asked my niece to apply to Cornell University, Columbia University, and Wellesley College in New England, the first words out of her mouth were "Uncle, I will never get in. And how will I ever find the money to pay for it?" My advice to her was to focus on getting admitted—which meant putting together the best application package—and then worry about how it would get paid. The financial aid application is guaranteed to be successful if you do an excellent job on your application for admissions package.

Creating a financial aid file is the best way to get organized to complete a financial aid application. Make a file of all your financial documents and applications. Assemble all the necessary records of your family's earned income for the year, federal taxes paid for this year and the previous year, untaxed income received (social security benefits, etc.), money in checking and savings accounts, and records on value of current investments or owned business. These records will be very helpful as you sort out your financial aid applications and will also be helpful in verification of finances.

File all income tax returns (if required) as early as possible and request that your parents' employer's statements or bank statements be prepared, just in case verification of income becomes necessary. Also, remember to make photocopies of all financial aid documents that you submit and write your name and social security number (if you have one) on all of these documents. Provided you keep all documents organized and in a safe place, you have nothing to worry about; you'll be able to account for everything. Make sure that you take note of all financial aid deadlines and be sure to meet them, as financial aid is awarded on a "first come, first serve" basis.

10.1　FILLING OUT THE FORMS

10.1.1　U.S. Citizens Living Abroad

10.1.1.1　THE FAFSA (Free Application for Federal Student Aid)

Your application for federal aid begins with the FAFSA, a financial aid application that allows you to provide all necessary financial information—in the form of your SAR (Student Aid Report)—to the schools to which you are applying in order for them to determine your federal aid eligibility.

There are two ways in which you may apply:

(1) You may fill out and submit the FAFSA online at www.fafsa.ed.gov
(2) Request the paper version of the FAFSA from an educational agency. If you are unable to obtain this, you may write to the following address requesting that they send you a copy of the FAFSA application. Write to:

Federal Student Aid Information Center
P.O. Box 84
Washington, D.C. 20044

If you are submitting the FAFSA to the federal processing agency online, you can only do so after January 1st of the year in which you are applying. However, if you are submitting the paper version of the FAFSA, it is important that you request the FAFSA application ahead of time (approximately six weeks before the submission deadline) so you can meet all your financial aid deadlines on time.

10.1.1.2　Completing the FAFSA online

If you intend to file the FAFSA application online, your SAR may only be sent to up to six schools electronically, using each school's unique federal code. If you are applying to more than six schools, keep in mind the priority-filing deadlines of these schools. The earliest filing deadlines should be your first priority. For all the other schools that were not listed to receive your FAFSA results on the first FAFSA that you filed, you can still send your results. You do not need to file another FAFSA application. You may do one of the following two things:

STEP 10 - BEFORE YOU APPLY: The financial paperwork

(i) At www.fafsa.ed.gov you may make corrections to your submitted FAFSA. Go to the "Make Corrections" part of the application and replace the schools that have already received your FAFSA results with the ones you now want to receive your results. Then submit your "corrected" FAFSA.

(ii) After submitting the FAFSA online, you will be given a four-digit DRN (Data Release Number) unique to you, along with your Student Aid Report (SAR). You can request through e-mail that the rest of your schools (which were not listed on the FAFSA) use your DRN—XXXX—to access your Student Aid Report (SAR) online. Some schools may not be able to do this, in which case your only option will be (i) above.

Make sure that you have all the required documentation that you will need to fill out the FAFSA. It is a long application that will require time and patience. Also, you will want to sit with a parent to fill out the FAFSA, since their input will be greatly demanded.

In addition, make certain that you meet all financial aid requirements by specified deadlines. For instance, several state aid programs require that you fill out additional forms and private institutions may have their own specific deadlines as well. Your college's application deadline may be different than the deadlines for the above-mentioned financial aid sources. Take into account all specified deadlines. It is a good idea to submit the FAFSA after January 1st, prior to other imposed financial aid deadlines if this is at all possible.

After completing the FAFSA online request, a unique government pin number will be issued for yourself and for the parent who completed the FAFSA with you at the government pin site. Use the pin numbers that you will receive via e-mail to sign your completed FAFSA electronically.

You also have the option of printing out and mailing the FAFSA signature page after submitting the FAFSA online. Your FAFSA will not be considered complete without the required signatures, so make sure that you and one of your parents (the one who helped you fill out the FAFSA) sign the signature page.

10.1.1.3 After submitting the FAFSA

Once you have submitted your completed FAFSA application, the federal processing agency will take between 3-6 weeks to process your application and send you a detailed copy of your results on your Student Aid Report (SAR) through the mail. You may be asked to confirm or correct information on some forms and then return them to be processed again. The Student Aid Report (SAR) compares all your data and generates a Student Aid Index number (which allows you to know whether you've qualified for a Pell Grant) and an EFC (Expected/Estimated Family Contribution) number, which will be used to determine whether you qualify for campus-based aid programs like FSEOG, Federal Perkins Loans, and Federal Work-Study programs.

At www.fafsa.ed.gov you can complete and submit the FAFSA online, make corrections to your submitted FAFSA, and view your Student Aid Report. If you need help completing the FAFSA, you may go to www.ed.gov/prog-info/SFA/FAFSA.

10.1.1.4 THE CSS FINANCIAL AID PROFILE

The CSS (College Scholarship Service) Profile application is a financial aid application that consists of questions required of the schools and scholarship programs to which you are applying. The CSS Profile gives various institutions an idea of your financial situation in a single application and enables the colleges, universities, professional schools and scholarship programs you selected to award non-federal forms of financial aid. Some schools may not require the submission of the CSS Profile application. A complete list of colleges, universities and scholarship programs that require the Profile can be found online at www.collegeboard.com.

You can either complete the paper version of the Profile application and mail it or complete it online at www.collegeboard.com. If you decide to complete the paper version of the Profile, be sure to request it from the schools to which you are applying, or from any educational agency nearby that distributes the Profile application. For instance, U.S.I.S. may have these forms available. However, the fastest, most convenient way to complete the CSS/Financial Aid Profile is via the Internet at www.collegeboard.com

10.1.1.5 Completing the CSS Profile online

This is a two-step process:

(1) Registering for the application
(2) Applying

Keep in mind that registering for the Profile application requires an application fee, which means that you will need a valid credit card at hand.

The Profile registration fee of $5.00 covers the cost of preparing and mailing your Profile application. The additional fee of $17.00 for each school/program covers the costs involved in processing and reporting your Profile information to the schools you requested to receive your Profile application (using a unique four-digit school code).

It is important that you **register** at least four (4) weeks before the earliest school priority filing deadline: that is the date the school tells you that the College Board or the processing agency must receive your Profile application. In addition to this, it is important that you **submit** the Profile application to the College Board at least one week prior to the priority-filing dates specified by your schools, because it takes about one week—from the time the College Board receives your Profile application online—for the information you provide to be delivered to the schools and scholarship programs that you requested receive this information.

*If you are submitting the paper version of the Profile, it must be done two weeks prior to the priority filing deadlines of your schools. Note, however, that if you choose to complete the paper version of the Profile, it is best to deliver it to the CSS processing agency by express mail.

When applying for the Profile online, you will be instructed to download the applicable supplemental forms—the Business/Farm Supplement and/or the Non-custodial Parent's Statement—if necessary. However, if you decide to use the paper version of the application, these forms will be included in your Profile packet.

The Non-custodial Parent's Supplement

Even if your parents are divorced or separated, each of them is expected to contribute towards the cost of your college education. The parent with whom you have been living (your custodial parent) is the one expected to complete the PROFILE and the FAFSA with you, and the other parent (non-custodial parent) is to complete and submit the Non-custodial Parent's Supplement as part of the Profile application. If your custodial parent has remarried, his/her income and your step-parent's income (if you have a step-parent), should be documented on the Profile, as well as on the FAFSA.

The Business/Farm Supplement

This should be completed if either of your parents are self-employed or own a business/farm.

Remember to take note of the deadlines for submission of the CSS/Profile. Early decision candidates using the paper version of the Profile must register with the College Scholarship Service (CSS) early and must submit the Profile application form to CSS early, and if applicable, submit the Non-custodial Parent form and/or Business/Farm Supplement information along with it.

10.1.1.6 After submitting the Profile application

After submitting your Profile application to the College Board, you should receive acknowledgement within 2-3 weeks. When the financial aid office of the institution to which you are applying, receives the Profile information from CSS (College Scholarship Service), they will make an analysis of your family's financial aid eligibility, based on their own need-based formula. They will use the Profile to determine whether or not you qualify for institutional financial assistance, as well as estimate your federal financial aid eligibility.

If you have any questions regarding the CSS/Profile, send an e-mail to help@CSSprofile.org

Remember that the information you provide and which passes between the College Board and you is confidential. This information, along with the credit card number you provide, is encrypted, so data transmitted along the Internet is secure.

10.1.1.7 Other Required Documentation

Some schools may require that you submit the following documents as part of your financial aid application:

1. **Signed student and parent federal income tax returns for the previous year**

If you and/or your parents do not file tax returns, bring this to the attention of the financial aid office of the school(s) to which you are applying. They might have you and/or your parents submit a non-tax filer form, or you might be required to submit some other financial aid documentation in lieu of this so they can waive this requirement for you.

2. Parents' and student's W-2 forms and schedules

Being a U.S. citizen living abroad, the W-2 forms and schedules—much like the federal income tax returns—may not be applicable to you. In which case, you must explain to the financial aid offices of the schools to which you are applying that you are a U.S. citizen living abroad and that your parents live and work abroad (if this is the case), and that these requirements are not applicable to you. After receiving a rational explanation of your special circumstance, the schools will waive these requirements for you.

10.1.2 International Students

If you are a non-U.S. citizen or you are not a permanent resident of the U.S., you must follow different criteria than U.S. citizens living abroad when completing your financial aid application. As an international student, you are most likely not required to complete and submit the FAFSA as well as the Profile application. Most schools require **all** applicants to submit their applications for need-based and/or merit-based financial aid. In addition to, or in place of the school's general application for financial aid, you may be asked to submit a separate financial aid application for international students.

Available at www.collegeboard.com is the **College Scholarship Service's Foreign Student Financial Aid Application.** Some schools may require international students to submit this application. Various schools also require international applicants to complete a Declaration and Certification of Finance form. (Schools which do not offer financial aid to international students often request this.)The Declaration and Certification of Finances is needed in order for these schools to complete an I-20 form, which is used to obtain a student F-1 visa, should you decide to enroll.

It is advisable to attach documentation of family income to your financial aid application. Ask your parents to obtain a certified bank statement from their bank(s); make sure to indicate your current exchange rate in U.S. dollar amounts. A copy of your parents' employers' statements of income earned will also suffice.

Check it out

Checking out the financial aid policies of the various schools to which you intend to apply should be your first priority as you begin the financial aid application process. You must also keep in mind that in some schools need-based financial aid is offered only to U.S. citizens and permanent residents of the U.S., and not to international students. These schools may ask international students to cover the cost of their education without institutional aid, in which case you—as an international student—may need to complete a Declaration of Finances, or I-20 form. Other schools, however, may offer financial aid to all of their applicants.

Check with each institution and find out whether you are eligible for the kind of financial aid you are seeking. Many schools offer payment plans and loans to international students who need it.

10.2 FINANCIAL AID RESOURCES

Learn as much as you can about financial aid by exploring all the resources available to you. You'll be surprised what information is actually out there. Everything from where you can find the cheapest buys (money-wise) in a college education to all the sources of aid available to suit your particular needs.

Ask your school counselor or advisor for recommended books, and visit some financial aid websites. The United States Information Services (U.S.I.S.) library is also an invaluable source of information.

Here are some great financial aid websites you can visit:

- www.finaid.org here you can use an online calculator to estimate your EFC (Expected Family Contribution), use a scholarship search database and more
- The U.S. Department of Education's www.ed.gov/studentaid-links for information on federal sources of financial aid

There are also a number of websites that provide a great amount of information about **international** admissions and financial aid:

- Institute of International Education: www.iie.org
- NAFSA, Association of International Education: www.nafsa.org
- edu PASS: www.edupass.org
- International Education Financial Aid: www.iefa.org
- European Council of International Schools: www.ecis.org/colleges/aid:htm

TO-DO ITEMS:

- Complete the financial aid application and submit it at least 3 weeks before the deadline
- Request for financial aid based on need. Merit-based aid will be awarded based on how strong your application for admission is relative to other applicants.

- STEP 11 -
THE INTERVIEW AND THE FOLLOW-UP

This is your chance to tell your story live and put a face behind the vision

11.1   THE INTERVIEW

While some schools do not require an interview as part of your application, many strongly encourage that you do have one. The interview helps admission officers get a better picture of the person behind the application. It offers them a personal perspective and a chance to put a face behind your story and the vision you aspire to. Your interpersonal skills, the passion with which you talk about your goals, and your enthusiasm for the school are the things you seek to convey to the colleges during the interviews.

Most colleges make on-campus interviews available to prospective students throughout the summer and fall of the applicant's senior year in secondary or high school. In many such cases, colleges will schedule interviews with a representative or alumni near your hometown.

Appointments for these interviews may be scheduled through the admission offices. If you are able to make a trip to an on-campus interview, then take advantage of that opportunity. An on-campus interview can go a long ways in demonstrating your seriousness in the college and give you an opportunity to see the place where you plan to spend your next few years. If you live in a foreign country, the United States Information Services (U.S.I.S.) agency office in your country may be a good place to check whether you can schedule an interview for the colleges to which you apply.

> **Counting on Alumni**
>
> Recent statistics show that prospective MIT students who have interviews with educational counselors are 2.3 times more likely to be admitted than those who don't. Scheduling face-to-face interviews with thousands of candidates is impossible for the admissions personnel, whose calendars are already jam-packed, so MIT dean of admissions Marilee Jones relies on more than 2,100 alumni volunteers around the world to meet with prospective students. The reports these educational counselors provide can have a huge influence on whether a student is offered admission or not. *– Technology Review*

11.1.1 Before the interview

Think of an interview as a conversation—not an inquisition—with your interviewer. Interviewers are *not* shrinks who want to delve deep into the crevices of your conscious and subconscious mind and find out if there is anything wrong with you. They just want to know a little bit more about you and aspects of you they may not already know. So be calm and enjoy the conversation, but still maintain a formal disposition.

Do not go to an interview session with no preparation. It is important that you go through a mock interview with a friend, a parent, a teacher, or a mentor playing the part of the interviewer.

Prepare for the interview about two days in advance. Start by putting together a folder of information on that particular college. Read the college's brochure, visit their websites, and read about their traditions and news stories. Review copies of the documents you have mailed to the school. Go over your essays and recant the vision you believe the college can help you realize. Finally, come up with 10 most likely questions you may be asked with regard to your reason for applying to that college. Spend the day before the interview doing mock interviews, where you allow the person role-playing the interviewer to grill you on these 10 questions and any others. The goal of these mock interviews is to help make you comfortable with answering the questions with confidence and clarity.

You know what you are looking for in a college education and you know what each college has to offer in light of the vision you seek for yourself. So look forward to these interviews with optimism and enthusiasm. That is what interviewers are looking for: enthusiasm to tell your story and demonstrate your passion for the college. Know what it is that you want to put across. Talk about your values and aspirations, about your interests and your goals. Speak clearly and concisely, straight to the point, like you know exactly what it is you desire in a college education. There is no room for doubt or unwarranted modesty. Above all, do not be afraid to ask questions if you are given the opportunity to do so.

11.1.2 Selling Yourself

Think of your colleges as job recruiters who want to see whether you fit the job. The admission officers who read your application would like to consider you, so sell yourself, and not at a cheap price! While you are applying to the colleges where you would like to spend the next four years of your life, admission officers are busy selecting students who they would like to be a part of their community. Think of yourself as the admission committees. In the end they are just like you, looking for the perfect match.

As admissions officers search for suitable matches for their school, first they use an objective criterion; they look at your standardized test scores, transcript, and your academic record in order to see whether they have a fit. This is basically the cut-off point. Secondly, they look at more personal characteristics that may be revealed in your essays or in your choice of extracurricular involvement. Whatever the case may be, they will assemble a class of students whom they think share commonalities, and who they also think will be able to contribute to the college community. They will choose individuals who have distinct paths and unique destinies to follow—who have differences that will embellish and enhance one another—and most of all those who greatly desire to be a part of their communities.

Remember that your application gives you the opportunity to distinguish yourself in any way that you so desire and allows you to have your voice heard by the admission staff. Do not sell yourself short; this is your time to tell the college what distinguishes you from the pack of applicants.

11.2 THE FOLLOW UP

After you have completed the admission and financial aid applications and mailed in all of your applications to the schools, it is time to relax—no more deadlines to meet. Enjoy the break and save your energy for the upcoming months, when you will be making some tough decisions.

After the receipt of your application materials, most schools will either mail you an acknowledgement card, a letter, or send you an e-mail stating that they have received your application. They will usually make available an "application status" section on their college websites which you can access using a unique code that will be given to you. You can check the status of your application on these sites and find out whether you have fulfilled all of the requirements.

Check your application status sites as often as possible, since required documents often get lost in the mail or misplaced. Do not be worried if you have recently sent in all the required documents, but you get repeated notices still asking for missing documents. Chances are that your schools have received them, but they are not on file yet. Often a phone call to the admissions office is all it takes to clear that up. If, however, it has been about a month and you have received no acknowledgement that they have your application or you have met all the requirements, make sure to inform your schools that there is a problem and get it straightened out as soon as possible. Mistakes are often made, and correcting those mistakes is an important part of the follow-up.

Note that it is very important to have photocopies of all the application materials you ever submitted, just in case they get lost in transit. If you have not done that yet, this is the time to go back and carefully review the folder you put together for each of the schools on your target list.

The form provided below is a good way to keep track of progress being made on each of the schools to which you applied.

Task	Timeline	Columbia University Status	Wellesley College Status	Stanford University Status	Columbia University Status
Draw Up Target List	June				
Request Application Forms	July	⬆	⬆	⬆	⬇
Complete Forms	August	⬆	⬇	⬆	⬇
Complete Required Essays	August	⬆	⬇	⬆	⬇
Register for SAT, TOEFL Tests	August	⇨	⬆	⬆	⬆
Have a professional writer review essays	September	⇨	⇨	⬆	⊗
Finish Supplemental Package	September	⇨	⊗	⇨	⇨
Submit Completed Applications	September			⬆	
Submit Primary Recommendations	September				
Submit Supplemental Recommendations	September				
Take Tests and Submit Results	October				
Interview or Visit	October				
Follow-up to make sure all requirements received	January				

Key:
Achieved Target ⬆
On Track To Achieve Target ⇨
Behind Schedule To Achieve Target ⬇
Not Applicable ⊗

The top of the form has a list of your chosen colleges, and the first column has a list of the different tasks that need to be completed for each school. Use the appropriate arrow to indicate the status of each task on each of the schools. For the schools that are behind schedule, pick up the phone or e-mail an admissions officer to find out the status. If you are behind in completing these tasks, ask for an extension from the admission's officer.

11.2.1 The Waiting Game

Once you have fulfilled all of the application requirements and your schools have notified you of this, you can sit comfortable. It's time to play the "waiting game."

Some schools may take a rather personalized approach to their applicants and correspond with them throughout the application process. With other schools, you may feel that you are not even recognized. Don't worry, this is not the case; they just prefer to keep things close to the vest. Now that you have some time to yourself, it's never too late to investigate your college choices some more. You might discover some new things.

Ask yourself; *is this school actually right for me?* Also ask yourself how well you think you will excel in each individual school. Visit college websites and explore them. Talk to current students and get an idea of what you might be looking forward to. Ask staff and students questions about anything from graduate placement opportunities available to campus and student life. What kind of sports opportunities would you like to take advantage of? What are some of the specific clubs and activities that you would like to a part of? Consider also whether the college has a strong alumni network; this is fundamental to career placement opportunities. Where have graduates gone after college? See if the college's profile matches yours and finds a place within your comfort zone; be selective.

All you can do now is wait to see which colleges accept you. It's out of your hands; right now *they're* making the decisions.

TO-DO ITEMS:

- Set up interview sessions with the school representatives at least 2 weeks in advance.
- Take a day to prepare for each interview.
- Send a "Thank You" note or card to the interviewer after each interview.

- STEP 12 -
THE FINAL DECISION

Expect the one decision that will make your vision close to a reality.

12.1   THE BIG FAT ENVELOPE OR THE THIN ONE

A few months after completing your applications and all requirements, you begin to wait in anticipation of a decision. Finally, the letters from the schools begin arriving in the mail. After the long wait, you are going to find out whether you have been granted or denied admission to the colleges to which you applied. Well, it is okay to be anxious in anticipation. You are probably looking at the envelope and saying "This is my fate" and waiting to tear it open. Relax, take a deep breath, and rip it open.

You will read one of three things. Either you have been accepted, denied admission altogether, or you have been placed on the waiting list (in which case you still have a chance of being accepted into the school of your choice). If you receive a big fat envelope from one of your schools in the mail, chances are you have been granted admission. These big envelopes usually contain an acceptance letter, a financial aid award letter, some forms you must fill out if you intend to enroll in that particular institution, and some other information about the school.

By now you probably know which college is your first choice. Cross your fingers and hope they have accepted you. Do not write off all the other schools to which you applied, just in case your first choice denied you admission or placed you on their waiting list; other options are available to you. Most schools give applicants who have been accepted about a month to respond to the acceptance letter (for most schools the deadline for applicant response is May 1st).

If you were not accepted into your fist choice school, don't let it bother you. Many schools have a lot to offer, and in various ways. It's not the end of the world. Once you have received all of your admission letters, it is time for you to make a decision. This is the final draw. Where would you like to spend the next four years of your life? Where do you want to excel? Where do you feel comfortable? It is important to make the decision on your own; you're the one going off to college—not your dad, not your mom, not your college counselor or any other person, for that matter. Now would probably be a good time to follow that *gut* feeling. Don't worry; you'll make the right decision.

As soon as you have decided which college you would like to enroll at, let that college know before its response deadline (usually May 1st) and mail in all the required forms (the ones that you received in the acceptance package) as soon as possible. Be sure also to let the other colleges that accepted you know that you appreciate their time and effort in evaluating your application, but that you have made a decision to enroll at another institution. They'll appreciate this very much.

12.2 THE AWARD LETTER

Do you remember when you were busy filling out all of those financial aid applications? Well, it paid off. Once it has been confirmed that all of your financial aid application materials have been received, your schools will start preparing a financial aid package for you and notify you of this award in a letter—that is if you have been accepted into that particular institution.

If your decision to attend a particular institution will depend on whether or not you were offered a good financial aid award, you will have to carefully evaluate all of your aid offers. Are there any hidden costs? Are there too many loan components and not enough grants or scholarship aid? Are merit and scholarship awards renewable?

12.2.1 The Financial Aid Offer Letter

July 26, 2003   2003-2004 ACADEMIC YEAR

Mariam Okine   DUPLICATE NOTIFICATION
PO Box 1200
Accra, Ghana

The Office of Financial Aid and Student Employment has completed its review of your application for financial assistance. We are pleased to inform you that you have been awarded financial aid as described below. If you have any questions concerning your financial aid, please do not hesitate to contact our office.

[signature]

Thomas C. Keane
Director of Financial Aid and Student Employment

ESTIMATE OF COSTS:		ESTIMATE OF RESOURCES:	
Tuition	$28,754	Parents' Contribution	$0
Room & Board	9,580	Summer Savings Expectation	1,960
Books &Supplies	640	Student Assets	0
Personal Expenses/Travel	1,484	Other Resources	0
TOTAL BUDGET	$40,458	TOTAL FAMILY RESOURCES	$1,960
		FINANCIAL NEED	$38,498

TOTAL SCHOLARSHIP/GRANT AID (AS DETAILED BELOW)		$33,459
CORNELL UNIVERSITY GRANT	26,709	
FEDERAL PELL GRANT - ESTIMATE	4,000	
TOTAL SELF-HELP (AS DETAILED BELOW):		$5,035
WILLIAM D. FORD FEDERAL DIRECT SUBSIDIZED LO,	2,625	
FEDERAL PERKINS LOAN	610	
FEDERAL WORK STUDY (FWS) ELIGIBILITY	1,800	
TOTAL FINANCIAL AID PACKAGE:		$38,494

12.2.1.1 Comparing financial aid awards

If you applied for financial aid, your aid awards will vary from college to college. As you evaluate all of your aid offers, you might want to determine which is the greatest. To do this, first you need to subtract the amount of aid that you received from the comprehensive cost of attendance of your college. Some colleges may offer you a great bargain, but their cost of attendance may be high. Other colleges with a lower cost of attendance may offer the same amount of financial aid, making them relatively more affordable.

Consider also the components of your financial aid awards: loans, grants, scholarships, work study. Some aid awards may have numerous loan components, so once you leave school you will be in some heavy debt. It is important to compare loan interest rates and determine which ones are reasonable for you.

Once you have figured out the true costs involved in attending the college you are considering, you must reflect on the question of value. Indeed, cost is an important factor. What's more important, nonetheless, is which college best serves your purposes and future aspirations.

12.2.1.2 Assessing value

A good quality education does not come cheap. Yes, it is expensive. As you make your college choice, it is important to take into account not only the cost of your college education, but the value as well. College is an investment in your future, so why not pay for the best future possible? Think about the quality of education you want and decide what is important to you.

If you want to go to a certain college but the cost involved is too much, or you were offered better aid awards elsewhere, don't dismiss the chance of going to the college of your choice. After all, most financial aid offers are negotiable. Some colleges even offer to match up the better aid offers that you received if you are willing to accept their offer of admission. Contact the admission or financial aid offices to see whether their aid offers are negotiable, given your current financial situation. Some offers may be non-negotiable, but it won't hurt to ask.

Keep in mind that the longer you wait to make the final decision in choosing your college, the longer other students might have to wait for colleges to determine whether they have extra funds to distribute. Likewise, the longer it takes for colleges to establish whether they have an open space available for students on waiting lists. So play nice and don't keep colleges on the string!

Also, if you applied under the Early Decision Plan for one of your colleges and you were accepted into that college, you do not have the option of choosing which of the other colleges (that accepted you) you would like to attend. Remember? In your application you made a **binding agreement** to enroll, once offered admission.

TO-DO ITEMS:

- Discuss your application decisions and results with the individuals who wrote recommendation letters on your behalf
- Discuss all admission offers with your mentor, parents, and family
- Discuss offers with alumni from the school that admitted you, and decide

PUTTING IT ALL TOGETHER

What you have just gone through in this book are the 12 essential steps that take you through how to put together an effective application for admissions package. It is more than just an application for admissions. This package is your life's portfolio that carefully documents the story of who you are, what you are capable of, what you have to offer, your vision for your life and, most important, why the college you have chosen is the place to realize that vision. This package is your first opportunity ever, at this point in your life, to open the right door to see your vision unfold into reality.

These steps partly require you to focus your efforts on the details of the application and clearly distinguish yourself from the countless number of applicants who are competing with you for admission. Each step in the process should also encourage you to go that extra mile or do that extra work needed to successfully present yourself and your vision. My younger brother applied for admissions only at MIT, but at every step of the process he made every effort necessary to ensure success. He got admitted about the same time our neighborhood was having problems with a postal strike and mail being stolen. He traveled by himself for about two days to visit my eldest brother, who at the time was teaching in northern Nigeria, and then asked MIT to resend the admissions offer to him in Nigeria. Now, would the package have gotten lost if mailed to our home address? Nobody knows, but that was a risk he was not willing to take on his future—on him realizing his vision at MIT.

To conclude, I would like to remind you of the following pieces of advice. The points below are often lost in the details and can potentially derail a successful application.

- Read application instructions for all institutions carefully, especially since application criteria differ among various institutions

- Be sure to print your name and social security number, if you have one, on all of your submitted documents (essays, financial aid forms, creative works, and supplemental works), so admission and financial aid officers can track these documents

- Keep copies of all your documents in organized application folders: one for admission documents and one for financial aid documents

- Pay attention to deadlines and make sure required documents or communication are submitted on time. Need-based and merit-based aid can only be guaranteed to applicants who meet financial aid deadlines.

- Be sure to make a checklist of each of your school's application deadlines. Once you have completed an application and you are ready to mail it, make sure to write down the exact date on which you mailed it, so that if there is any uncertainty as to whether you mailed in a particular document you can always check.

- It is very important to have Internet access and an e-mail account, if at all possible. Using e-mail to communicate with the school can help alleviate problems you may encounter with the postal service. Be sure to provide all of your schools with a valid e-mail address to which you will have access throughout the application process. Most urgent and time-sensitive correspondence about your application should be handled via e-mail.

- Be sure to have access to your mail—snail mail or e-mail—throughout the application process so you don't miss out on any critical deadlines and important notices or information.

- Keep contact information for all of your schools: e-mail addresses, fax numbers, telephone numbers. You should divide them into two categories: one for financial aid offices and one for admission offices. These will come in handy when you want to ask for extensions on application deadlines or notify your schools of discrepancies in information to have some of your questions answered.

- If you plan to fax information to any of your schools, it is important that you do so with a cover letter with your full name, social security number, and a short explanation of what you are faxing.

Getting successfully admitted to the school you choose is the ultimate first step in influencing your future. You successfully completed high school or secondary school, and that means you have been given the tools to define your vision for your life. You can almost get admitted to any school in the world without much effort. However, to get admitted to the school you choose, where your vision can become a reality and the day of your graduation can become a celebration for the rest of your life, takes careful planning. This book has given you all the tools you need, so use them.

APPENDIX - Worksheets

CREATING TARGET LIST

	Schools					My Preference	Rating for My Preference
Size	❶					❷	1 Must have
Type of School							0 Not import
Location							-1 Against
Curriculum							
Faculty							Rating for Schools
Student Body, Social Scene							4 excellent
Extracurricular Life							3 very good
Resources							2 good enough
Admission Requirements							1 not favorable
Financial Aid/Costs							

	Schools					
Size	= ❶ × ❷					
Type of School						
Location						
Curriculum						
Faculty						
Student Body, Social Scene						
Extracurricular Life						
Resources						
Admission Requirements						
Financial Aid/Costs						
Overall Score (Sum)						

FOLLOW-UP SHEET FOR TRACKING PROGRESS

Schools →					
Task	Timeline	Status	Status	Status	Status
Draw Up Target List	June				
Request Application Form	July				
Complete Forms	Aug.				
Complete Required Essays	Aug.				
Register for SAT, TOEFL Tests	Aug.				
Have a writer review essays	Sept.				
Finish Package	Sept.				
Submit Completed	Sept.				
Submit Primary Recommendatio	Sept.				
Submit other Recommendatio	Sept.				
Take Tests and Submit Results	Oct.				
Interview or Visit	Oct.				
Follow-up to make sure all received	Jan.				

Key:

Achieved Target ⬆

On Track to Achieve Target ➡

Behind Schedule to Achieve Target ⬇

Not Applicable ⊗

0-595-29647-5

CPSIA information can be obtained at www.ICGtesting.com
Printed in the USA
LVOW07s2353060316

478031LV00001B/260/P